Follow That Bee!

A First Book of Bees in the City

Scot Ritchie

Kids Can Press

To Katherine, who knows the beauty of a garden,
and the bees that come with it — S.R.

Kids Can Press gratefully acknowledges the financial support of the Government of Ontario, through the Ontario Media Development Corporation; the Ontario Arts Council; the Canada Council for the Arts; and the Government of Canada, through the CBF, for our publishing activity.

Published in Canada and the U.S. by Kids Can Press Ltd.
25 Dockside Drive, Toronto, ON M5A 0B5

Kids Can Press is a Corus Entertainment Inc. company

www.kidscanpress.com

The artwork in this book was rendered digitally.
The text is set in Futura.

Edited by Jennifer Stokes
Designed by Julia Naimska

Printed and bound in Malaysia, in 10/2018
by Tien Wah Press (Pte.) Ltd.

CM 19 0 9 8 7 6 5 4 3 2 1

MIX
Paper from
responsible sources
FSC® C012700

Library and Archives Canada Cataloguing in Publication

Ritchie, Scot, author, illustrator

    Follow that bee! : a first book of bees in the city / Scot Ritchie.

(Exploring our community ; 6)

Includes index.

ISBN 978-1-5253-0034-9 (hardcover)

1. Urban bee culture — Juvenile literature. 2. Bee culture — Juvenile literature. 3. Honeybee — Juvenile literature. 4. Honeybee — Social aspects — Juvenile literature. 5. Honeybee — Effect of human beings on — Juvenile literature. 6. Beekeepers — Juvenile literature. I. Title. II. Series: Ritchie, Scot . Exploring our community ; 6

SF523.5.R58 2019   j638'.1   C2018-901857-7

Contents

Meet the Bees

The five friends are buzzing with excitement today! They're visiting Martin's neighbor, Mr. Cardinal. He keeps beehives in his backyard and has invited everyone to see how honeybees live.

Mr. Cardinal

To bring more bees to urban spaces, many cities encourage people to build hives in their backyards.

4

School

Mr. Cardinal's House

Nick

Sally

Bee a Friend

Bees need flowers for food. And just like we need variety in our food, bees need to eat from a variety of flowers.

Mr. Cardinal gives his bees a helping hand by keeping a big garden with lots of different wildflowers. The five friends give Mr. Cardinal a helping hand by working in his garden.

Bees are suffering because they can't find the range of wildflowers they need. Pesticides and fungicides can also hurt bees. And when bees aren't strong and healthy, they may die from parasites and infections that normally wouldn't cause them harm.

Grow a Garden

Mr. Cardinal and the friends are heading to the garden center to look for more bee-friendly flowers to plant. Everyone wants to make sure that Mr. Cardinal's bees are well-fed!

Bees will travel many miles to find flowers, but they prefer to forage close to their hives. A bee might visit over a thousand flowers in one day!

Bees' Needs

At the garden center, everyone chooses native species — plants that are natural to the area. Bees like these the best. The kids load up the wagon with as many different bee-friendly plants as they can find.

Honeybees eat two things — and both are found in flowers. Nectar, which the bees turn into honey, is loaded with sugar and gives them energy. Pollen provides them with protein and fat.

Plant these, Help Bees!
Aster
Cilantro
Crocus
Fennel
Lavender
Poppy
Sage
Snowdrop
Sunflower
Thyme

Friends in Nature

Next, Mr. Cardinal takes the kids to a local pollinator garden.

"The flowers here are planted to attract pollinators like butterflies, bees and wasps," says Mr. Cardinal.

"What does a pollinator do?" asks Sally.

"A pollinator moves pollen from one flower or plant to another," says Mr. Cardinal.

One out of every three bites of food we eat comes from plants pollinated by bees. Without bees, there would be a lot fewer fruits, vegetables and nuts.

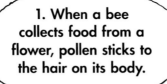

1. When a bee collects food from a flower, pollen sticks to the hair on its body.

2. When the bee goes to the next flower, the pollen it brings with it helps the flower to produce seeds.

3. The seeds then grow into new plants.

Honeycomb Home

"Look!" shouts Martin. "A beehive!"

Bees build their hives with wax that comes from their bellies. A female bee chews the wax, mixing it with her saliva, or spit. When she's done, it's just the right texture for building a wax cell. Rows of these cells make up a honeycomb. Many honeycombs make up a hive.

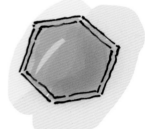

This six-sided shape is called a hexagon. It is the best shape for a honeycomb cell because it wastes no space and is super strong!

14

Let It Bee

Pedro notices a construction site next door. "That used to be an empty lot!"

As cities grow, many places that bees once called home are disappearing. But more and more cities are finding ways to get back to nature — people are turning their gardens and rooftops into homes for bees.

If an empty lot is left to nature, it will soon be full of bee-friendly flowers and plants.

Better Together

Back in Mr. Cardinal's yard, the friends watch the bees at work. In a hive, every bee has a job, and they work together. No one bee could survive on its own.

"They have chores to do around the house, just like we do!" says Pedro.

There is only one queen, and she's the biggest female in the colony. There are a few hundred drones in each hive, but there can be up to 80 000 worker bees.

A drone is a male bee. His job is to mate with the queen so that she can lay eggs.

The queen has only one thing to do — she lays eggs. And she can lay up to 2000 a day!
Worker bees are female, and they work the hardest. They collect pollen and nectar, make wax, clean the hive, feed the queen, care for the young and produce honey.

Bee or Not Bee?

Yulee notices that it isn't always easy to identify honeybees because other bugs — such as hornets, beetles and moths — can look similar. Mr. Cardinal teaches the five friends how to spot a honeybee.

Worker   Queen   Drone

A bee flaps its wings over 200 times a second. That's how a bee gets its buzz!

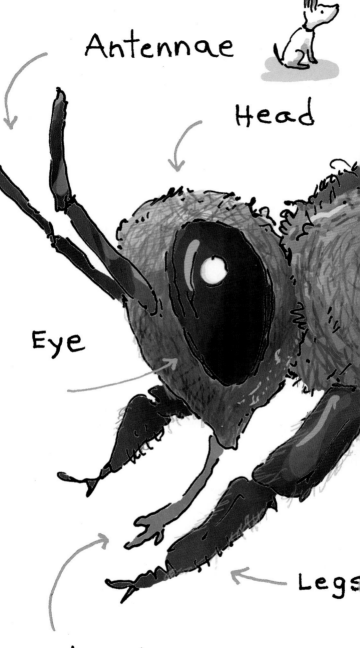

Antennae

Head

Eye

Proboscis

Legs

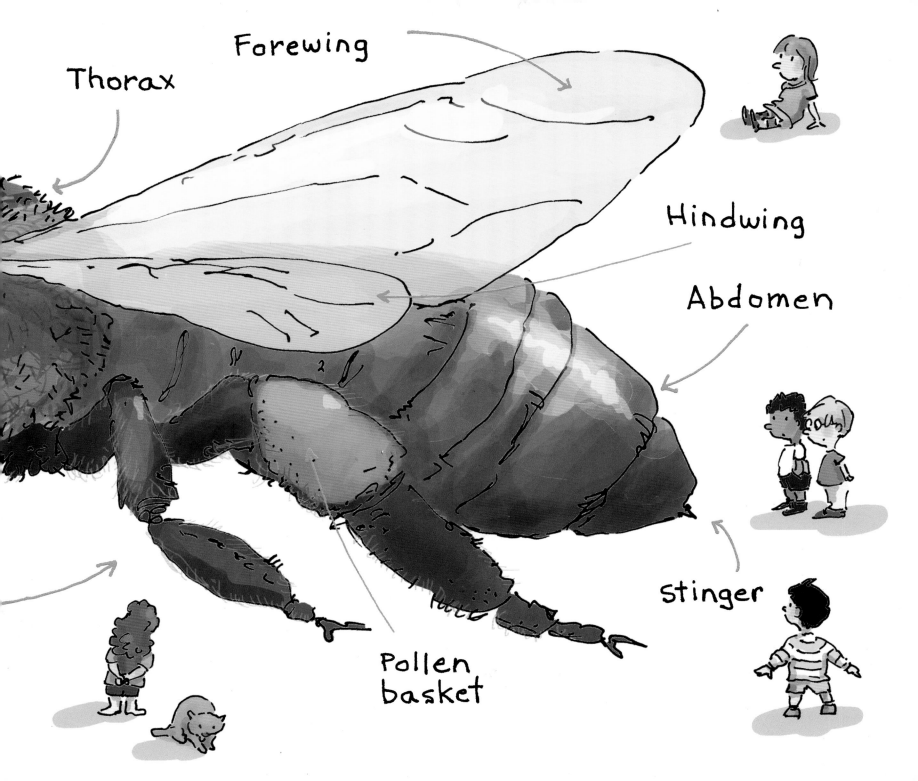

Forewing

Thorax

Hindwing

Abdomen

Stinger

Pollen
basket

Wiggle, Waggle!

Bees get excited, just like us. Sometimes they dance! When a bee comes back from foraging, she dances to tell the other bees where to find food. The round dance says there are flowers close by. The waggle dance says the flowers are far away and shows them which way to fly.

The direction and length of each waggle tells the other bees exactly where they can find pollen and nectar. The more a bee waggles, the more food is available!

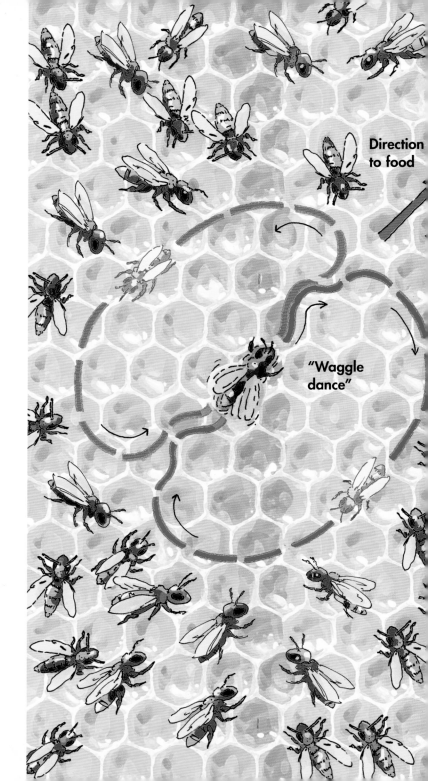

Direction to food

"Waggle dance"

Hey, That Stings!

"Ouch!" shouts Nick.

Bees sting to scare enemies away. A sting can be very painful for us, causing swelling, redness and itchiness — but it's much worse for the bee. After a bee stings you, its barbed stinger is torn away from its belly, and the bee dies.

Luckily, Mr. Cardinal knows what to do to help Nick. He pulls out the stinger as quickly as possible, washes the sting with soap and water, and applies ice. He explains that everyone should be extra careful around bees. Some people might be allergic to beestings and not be aware of it.

It's Honey Time!

Once a bee colony produces more honey than the bees need, the beekeeper can remove some. Beekeepers wear protective suits in case the bees sting them. Mr. Cardinal has another trick to protect himself.

"Smoke calms the bees," he says, as he takes the top off the hive.

Mr. Cardinal scrapes honey from the frame and puts it through a filter to remove the wax. Then the kids help him pour it into jars, ready for market!

A Buzzzy Day at the Market

Supporting local beekeepers, farmers and gardeners is one of the best ways you can help bees.

Is there a local market where you live?

Bee a Good Neighbor

Do you want to help the bees? Make a bee bath in your garden!

You'll need a shallow glass or ceramic dish; rocks, pebbles or marbles; and fresh water.

1. Put pebbles or small rocks inside the shallow dish. This gives the bees a place to stand while they drink.

2. Place the dish in a shady area of the garden.

3. Add water — just enough so the rocks are not covered.

Now your bees can drink, take water home to the larvae and cool their hives.

Don't forget to refill the water. A hive of bees can use a quart of water a day!

Does your school have a pollinator garden? Maybe you can start one. Be ready to spend time caring for the garden — plants need watering and pruning. And, remember, bees love dandelions.

Let nature take over! Plants will soon grow, and the bees will be grateful!

Words to Know

beesting allergy: when a person's immune system reacts to a beesting as though it were extremely harmful. A person having an allergic reaction to a beesting might experience wheezing, a swollen tongue or swollen lips, hives, dizziness, vomiting or loss of consciousness.

colony: a family of bees, including a queen, drones and workers

forage: to search for food

fungicide: a chemical used to kill fungus that harms plants

hive: the home where a bee colony lives

infection: when bad germs invade a body, causing disease and sickness

larvae: baby bees, before they transform into honeybees

native species: a plant that naturally grows in an area and has not been brought from another part of the world

nectar: the sugary liquid inside a flower

parasite: a living thing that lives and feeds on another living thing, often causing harm

pesticide: a chemical used to kill insects that are pests

pollen: a powdery substance that is transferred from one flower to another to make more flowers

pollination: the act of moving pollen from one flower to another

pollinator: an animal, such as a honeybee, bat or butterfly, that transfers pollen from flower to flower